PRESENTS

learn
Rock Guitar

INTERMEDIATE

Method by John McCarthy

Written and Adapted by Steve Gorenberg

Supervising Editor: Joe Palombo
Production Manager: Tara Altamuro
Layout, Graphics and Design: Steve Gorenberg
Photography: Nick Finelli
Audio Engineer: Jimmy Rutkowski

Copy Editors and Proofreaders:
Alex Palombo, Irene Villaverde

Cover Art Direction and Design:
Paul Enea, Tovero & Marks

ISBN: 978-0-9789832-4-6

Table of Contents

About the Author

John McCarthy
Creator of
the Rock House Method

John is the creator of **The Rock House Method**®, the world's leading musical instruction system. Over his 20 year career, he has produced and/or appeared in more than 100 instructional products. Millions of people around the world have learned to play music using John's easy to follow, accelerated program.

John is a virtuoso guitarist who has worked with some of the industry's most legendary musicians. He has the ability to break down, teach and communicate music in a manner that motivates and inspires others to achieve their dreams of playing an instrument.

As a guitarist and songwriter, John blends together a unique style of Rock, Metal, Funk and Blues in a collage of melodic compositions, jam-packed with masterful guitar techniques. His sound has been described as a combination of vintage guitar rock with a progressive, gritty edge that is perfectly suited for today's audiences.

Throughout his career, John has recorded and performed with renowned musicians like Doug Wimbish (who has worked with Joe Satriani, Living Colour, The Rolling Stones, Madonna, Annie Lennox and many more top flight artists), Grammy winner Leo Nocentelli, Rock & Roll Hall of Fame inductees Bernie Worrell and Jerome "Big Foot" Brailey, Freekbass, Gary Hoey, Bobby Kimball, David Ellefson (founding member of seven time Grammy nominee Megadeth), Will Calhoun (who has worked with B.B. King, Mick Jagger and Paul Simon), Jordan Giangreco from the acclaimed band The Breakfast, and solo artist Alex Bach. John has also shared the stage with Blue Oyster Cult, Randy Bachman, Marc Rizzo, Jerry Donahue, Bernard Fowler, Stevie Salas, Brian Tichy, Kansas, Al Dimeola and Dee Snyder.

For more information on John, his music and his instructional products visit www.rockhousemethod.com.

CREATING MUSICIANS
ONE LESSON AT A TIME

Introduction

Welcome to **The Rock House Method**® system of learning. You are joining millions of aspiring musicians around the world who use our easy-to-understand methods for learning to play music.

Unlike conventional learning programs, **The Rock House Method**® is a four-part teaching system that employs DVD, CD and 24/7 online lesson support along with this book to give you a variety of sources to assure a complete learning experience. The products can be used individually or together. The DVD that comes with this book matches the curriculum exactly, providing you with a live instructor for visual reference. In addition, the DVD contains some valuable extras like sections on changing your strings, guitar care and an interactive chord library. The CD that we've included lets you take your lessons with you anywhere you go.

How to Use the Lesson Support Site

Every Rock House product offers FREE membership to our interactive Lesson Support site. Use the member number included with your book to register at www.rockhousemethod.com. You will find your member number on the sleeve that contains your DVD and CD. Once registered, you can use this fully interactive site along with your product to enhance your learning experience, expand your knowledge, link with instructors, and connect with a community of people around the world who are learning to play music using **The Rock House Method**®. There are sections that directly correspond to this product within the *Additional Information* and *Backing Tracks* sections. There are also a variety of other tools you can utilize such as *Ask The Teacher, Quizzes, Reference Material, Definitions, Forums, Live Chats, Guitar Professor* and much more.

Icon Key

Throughout this book, you'll periodically notice the following icons. They indicate when there are additional learning tools available on our support website for the section you're working on. When you see an icon in the book, visit the member section of www.rockhousemethod.com for musical backing tracks, additional information and learning utilities.

CD Track Number

The accompanying CD includes lesson demonstrations, additional information and bass and drum backing tracks. When you see a CD icon and track number, follow along with the included CD to hear the examples and play along. A complete track listing is also included in the back of this book.

Backing Track

Many of the exercises in this book are intended to be played along with bass and drum rhythm tracks. This icon indicates that there is a backing track available for download on the Lesson Support Site.

Additional Information

The question mark icon indicates there is more information for that section available on the website. It can be theory, more playing examples, or tips.

Metronome

Metronome icons are placed next to the examples that we recommend you practice using a metronome. You can download a free, adjustable metronome from our support site.

Tablature

This icon indicates that there is additional guitar tablature available on the website that corresponds to the lesson. There is also an extensive database of music online that is updated regularly.

Tuner

Also found on the website is a free online tuner that you can use to help you tune your instrument.

Tablature Explanation

Tablature (or *tab*) is a number system for reading notes on the neck of a guitar. It does not require you to have knowledge of standard music notation. Most music for guitar is available in tab.

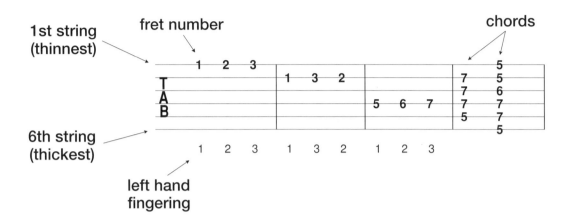

Techniques

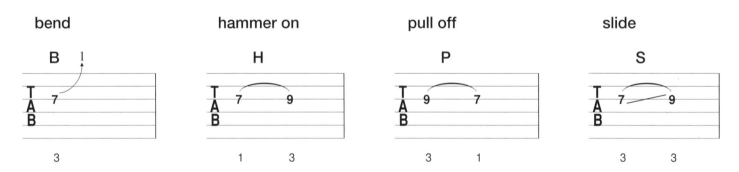

bend   hammer on   pull off   slide

Picking Symbols

   ⊓ - downstrum (strum down toward the floor)

   ∨ - upstrum (strum up toward the ceiling)

Lesson 1
Review Open Chords

Major Open Chords

A

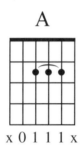

x 0 1 1 1 x

B

x x 2 3 4 1

C

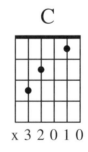

x 3 2 0 1 0

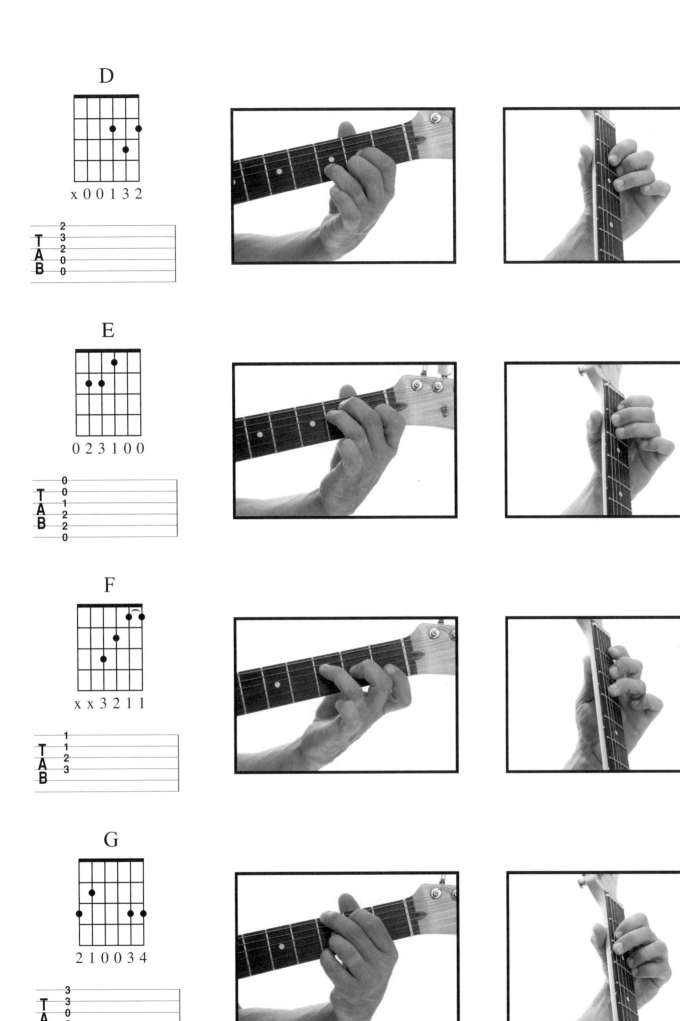

Minor Open Chords

Am

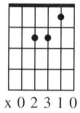

x 0 2 3 1 0

Bm

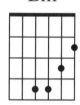

x x 3 4 2 1

Cm

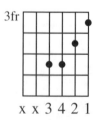

3fr

x x 3 4 2 1

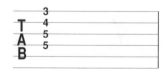

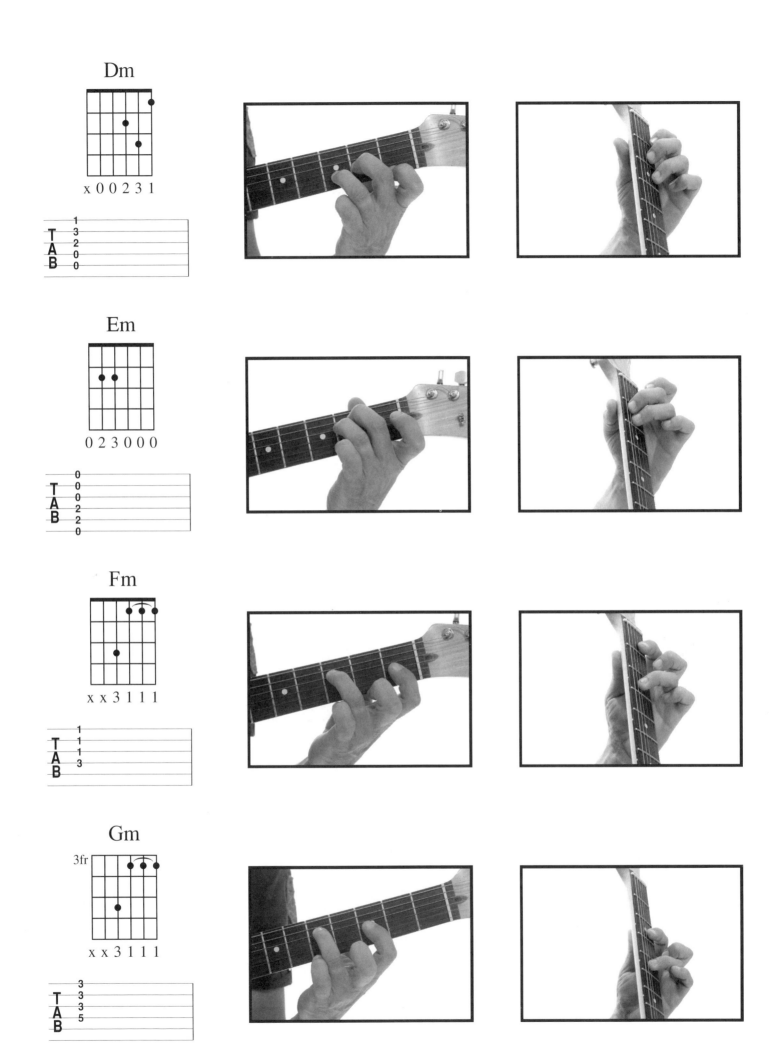

Lesson 2

Review Pentatonic Scales

Minor pentatonic scales are the most commonly used scales for playing rock and blues solos. The pentatonic scale is a five note scale, or an abbreviated version of the full natural minor scale. The word "pentatonic" comes from the greek words, "penta" (five) and "tonic" (the keynote). The following chart shows the notes in the A natural minor scale and the A minor pentatonic scale. The minor pentatonic is comprised of the 1st, 3rd, 4th, 5th and 7th steps of the natural minor scale. The first step (or note) of a scale is referred to as the *root note*. The root note is the note that gives a scale or chord its letter name. The root note of the A natural minor scale and the A minor pentatonic scale is the note A.

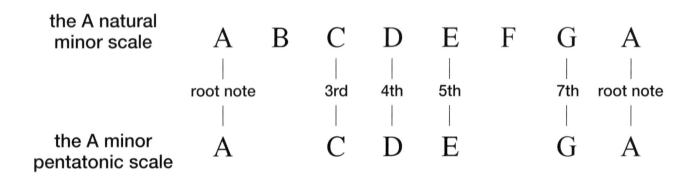

Memorize and practice this scale; it's the one you'll use most often for playing melodies and leads. There are five different positions of this scale, each beginning on a different note of the scale. All five positions are shown here in tab. To the right of each tab staff is a scale diagram. Suggested fingerings are shown beneath the tab staffs and scale diagrams, and the root notes (all of the A's) have been circled for your reference.

1st Position A Minor Pentatonic Scale

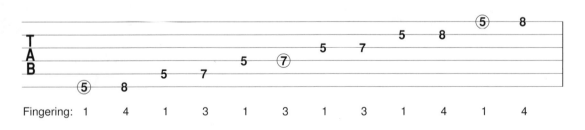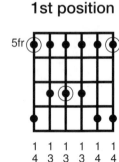

2nd Position A Minor Pentatonic Scale

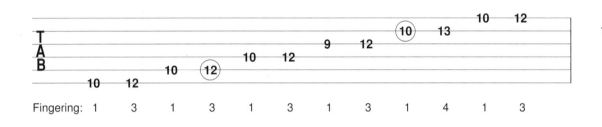

Fingering: 2   4   1   4   1   4   1   3   2   4   2   4

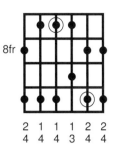

2nd position

8fr

2 1 1 1 2 2
4 4 4 3 4 4

3rd Position A Minor Pentatonic Scale

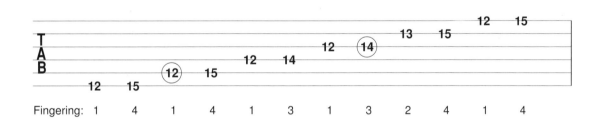

Fingering: 1   3   1   3   1   3   1   3   1   4   1   3

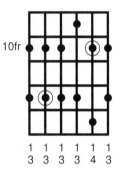

3rd position

10fr

1 1 1 1 1 1
3 3 3 3 4 3

4th Position A Minor Pentatonic Scale

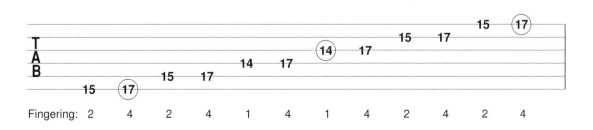

Fingering: 1   4   1   4   1   3   1   3   2   4   1   4

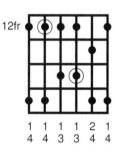

4th position

12fr

1 1 1 1 2 1
4 4 3 3 4 4

5th Position A Minor Pentatonic Scale

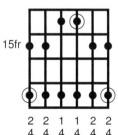

Fingering: 2   4   2   4   1   4   1   4   2   4   2   4

5th position

15fr

2 2 1 1 2 2
4 4 4 4 4 4

Minor Pentatonic Scale Fretboard Diagram

Once you have all five positions of the minor pentatonic scales mastered, you'll be able to play solos in any position on the neck. Remember that there are only five different name notes in the scale, and the different positions are just groupings of these same notes in different octaves and different places on the neck. The 4th and 5th positions from the previous page can be transposed one octave lower (shown below in the fretboard diagram). Notice how each positon overlaps the next; the left side of one position is the right side of the next one and so on. Think of these scale positions as building blocks (like Legos). When soloing, you can move from position to position and play across the entire fretboard. Memorize where all of the circled root notes are and think of them as your home base, or tonal center.

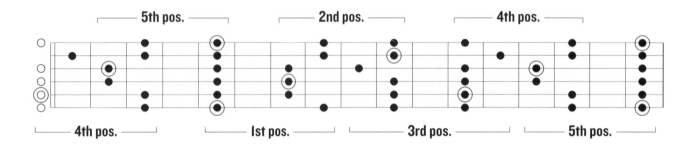

Lesson 3

Lead Patterns

The following examples are standard lead pattern exercises, designed to help you build coordination and learn how to begin using the minor pentatonics for playing leads. Use alternate picking and the metronome to start out slowly and get the rhythm. Memorize the patterns and gradually speed up the tempo. Before you know it, you'll be playing blazing rock and blues guitar solos.

Triplet Lead Pattern (1st Position)

Here is the 1st position A minor pentatonic scale played in groups of three notes, or triplets.
Count "one - two - three, one - two - three" out loud while you play through this exercise
to get the triplet feel in your head.

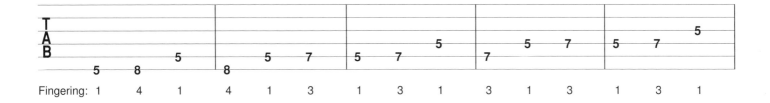

Fingering: 1   4   1   4   1   3   1   3   1   3   1   3   1   3   1

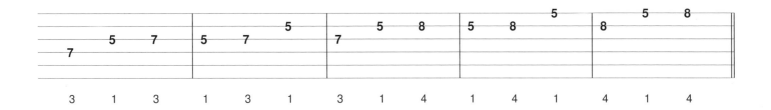

3   1   3   1   3   1   3   1   4   1   4   1   4   1   4

Now let's play the same pattern in reverse, back down the scale in triplets.

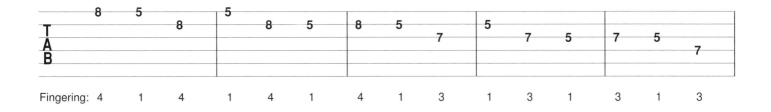

Fingering: 4   1   4   1   4   1   4   1   3   1   3   1   3   1   3

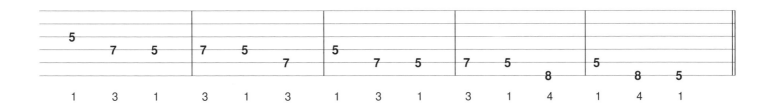

1   3   1   3   1   3   1   3   1   3   1   4   1   4   1

Triplet Lead Pattern (2nd Position)

Practice every position of the A minor pentatonic scale using the tripet lead pattern and alternate picking. The 2nd position ascending and descending triplet patterns are shown below. You can find more examples of lead patterns on the Lesson Support Site.

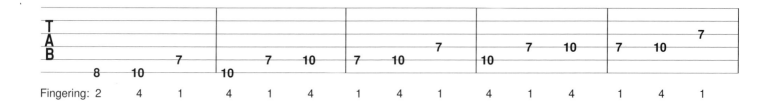

Fingering: 2 4 1 4 1 4 1 4 1 4 1 4 1 4 1

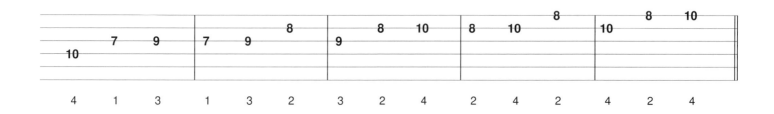

4 1 3 1 3 2 3 2 4 2 4 2 4 2 4

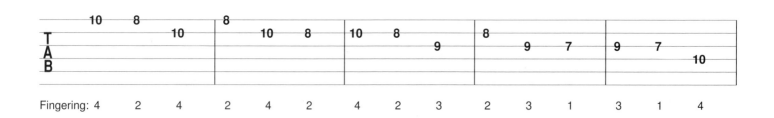

Fingering: 4 2 4 2 4 2 4 2 3 2 3 1 3 1 4

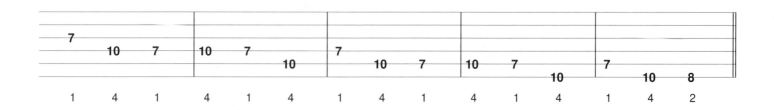

1 4 1 4 1 4 1 4 1 4 1 4 1 4 2

Hammer On & Pull Off Lead Pattern (1st Position)

The next lead pattern is a little more complex and uses a three note combination hammer on and pull off within each measure. Pick only the first note of each hammer on and pull off phrase, indicated by a slur above the tab staff. For each of these phrases, fret and hold the first note, then hammer on to the second note and pull off back to the original note in one smooth motion. The fingering underneath the staff shows you which left hand fingers to use for each hammer on and pull off combination.

The first two tab staffs show the pattern ascending through the 1st position of the A minor pentatonic scale. The next two staffs descend through the same position, using a slightly different rhythm and phrasing. As before, start out practicing slowly along with a metronome and build up speed gradually. Once you've got it down, try to experiment with different patterns and rhythms and come up with some of your own ideas.

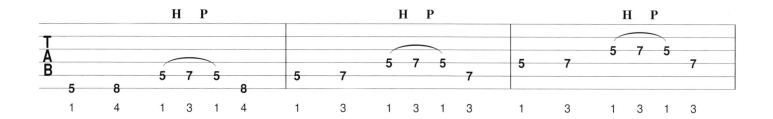

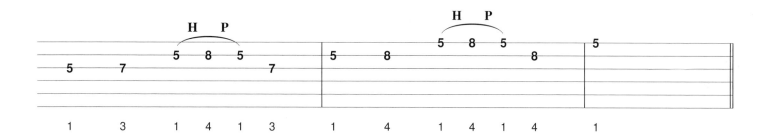

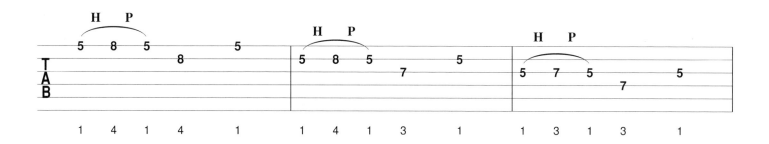

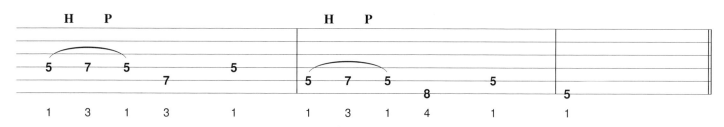

Hammer On & Pull Off Lead Pattern (2nd Position)

Here's the same hammer on & pull off pattern shown in the 2nd position. This one may seem slightly harder to play because the frets are farther apart in the 2nd position. Playing this pattern in all five positions will give you a great workout and help build up endurance in your left hand.

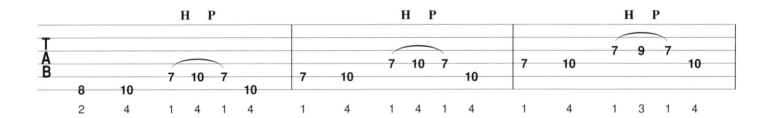

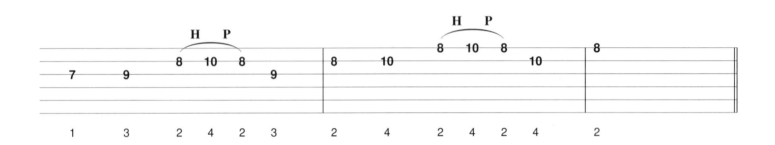

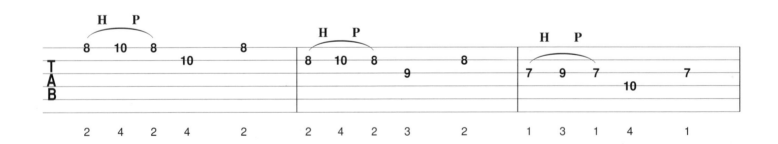

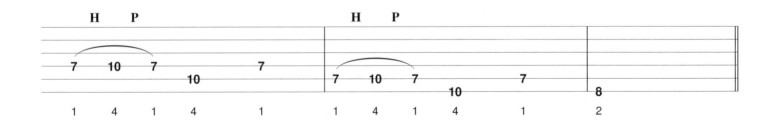

Lesson 4

Bending Exercise

The following three riffs utilize different bending techniques in the context of a lead. Each riff uses the A minor pentatonic scale in a different position. These are just a few examples of how to use bending techniques in the context of scales and leads using different left hand fingers.

The first riff is played in the 1st position of the scale and contains a few examples of the bend and release technique. To bend and release, bend the note up to the correct pitch, then release the bend and bring the note back to its original pitch without picking the string again. When performing fourth finger bends, use all of your other left hand fingers behind the fretted note to help push up and control the pitch of the bend.

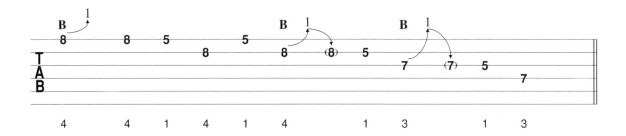

This next riff is played in the 2nd position and contains a first finger bend. This bend is slightly more difficult because you need to push up on the string using only one finger. Listen to the pitch of the bend to make sure you're pushing the string up far enough and the resulting note doesn't fall flat.

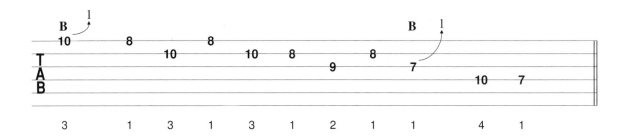

The third riff is played in the 4th position at the 12th fret and contains a second finger bend. The squiggly line at the end of this riff is an example of vibrato. Vibrato is the small, fast shaking of a note. While sustaining the note, shake your finger slightly and "dig in" to the note to slightly vibrate the pitch and give it more expression. Vibrato can also be applied while bending a note.

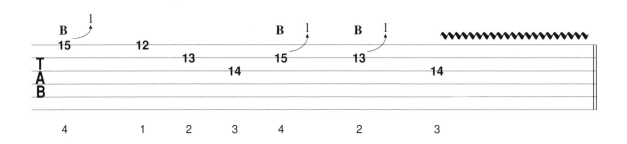

Lesson 5

Barre Chords

Let's begin this section by expanding your chord vocabulary. The following full barre chords contain no open strings, so they are *moveable* chords; you can transpose them to any fret. After mastering these chords, you'll be able to play in any key and position on the guitar.

6th String Barre Chords

The first chord is F major. This chord is especially difficult to play because you need to barre across all six strings with your first finger, then add the other three notes as well. Pick out each note individually to make sure the chord sounds clean.

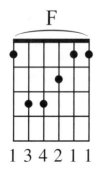

1 3 4 2 1 1

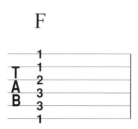

Notice that the lowest note of the chord is F, the *root note*. Using the musical alphabet, you can move barre chords up the neck and change them to any chord in the scale. Use the following chart to find any chord along the 6th string by moving the F chord. The name of the chord will change depending on which fret you move the chord to.

6th string notes (F chord)	E	F	F♯	G	G♯	A	A♯	B	C	C♯	D	D♯	E
fret number	Open	1	2	3	4	5	6	7	8	9	10	11	12

Once you've learned the F barre chord, simply lift your second finger and you'll have the Fm barre chord. The F7 (also called the *F dominant seventh*) barre chord is only slightly different from the F as well; just reposition your fourth finger and you've got it. Dominant seventh chords are often used in blues as substitutes for major chords.

Fm

1 3 4 1 1 1

Fm

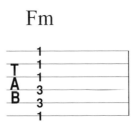

```
T   1
    1
A   1
    3
B   3
    1
```

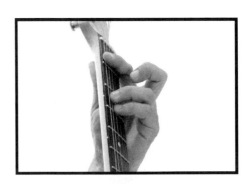

F7

1 3 1 2 4 1

F7

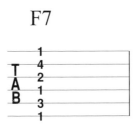

```
    1
T   4
    2
A   1
B   3
    1
```

21

5th String Barre Chords

The B♭ major barre chord is played at the 1st fret with the root note on the 5th string. This chord has a third finger barre. Make sure the 1st and 6th strings are muted and not strummed. Use the chart below to transpose this chord to any other fret along the 5th string.

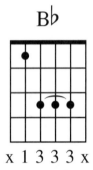

x 1 3 3 3 x

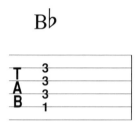

5th string notes (B♭ chord)	A	B♭	B	C	C#	D	D#	E	F	F#	G	G#	A
fret number	Open	1	2	3	4	5	6	7	8	9	10	11	12

The B♭m and B♭7 barre chords are played using a first finger barre. Once you have them mastered, try transposing both chords to other frets using the 5th string chart on the previous page.

B♭m

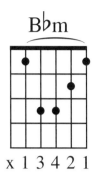

x 1 3 4 2 1

B♭m

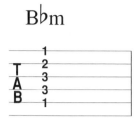

```
   1
T  2
A  3
B  3
   1
```

B♭7

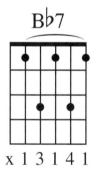

x 1 3 1 4 1

B♭7

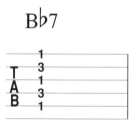

```
   1
T  3
A  1
B  3
   1
```

Lesson 6

Rhythms To Play Scales & Patterns Over

Open Chord Rhythm & Lead

This chord progression combines both major and minor chords in the key of A minor. The four chords used in the progression are shown in order using chord diagrams below. Use the alternate fingering for the Em chord (with your first and second fingers) to make changing from chord to chord easier. Notice how similar the fingerings are between the Am and C chords; simply move your third finger and leave your other fingers stationary. Play along with the backing track and practice changing chords cleanly and in time. Use the strumming pattern indicated by the symbols above the tab staff.

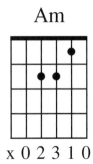 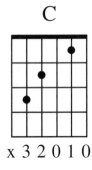 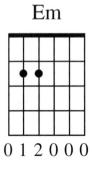 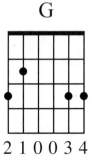

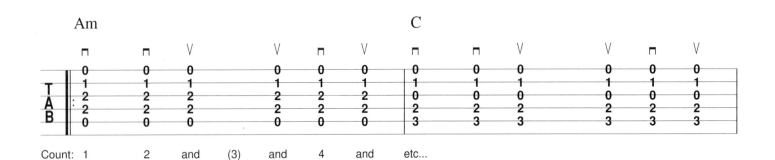

Once you've got the rhythm down, you can practice playing lead patterns and scales along with the backing track. You can use all five positions of the A minor pentatonic scale to improvise and try changing from position to position cleanly and in time. Start out by playing the triplet lead pattern or the hammer on and pull off pattern, then mix it up and experiment to come up with your own ideas. The following example lead ican be played over the Open Chord Rhythm. The chord symbols have been included above the staff as a reference. Play through this example to get some ideas, then make up your own leads.

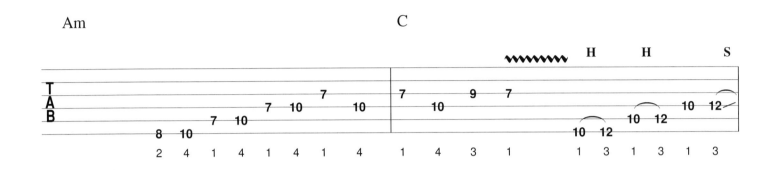

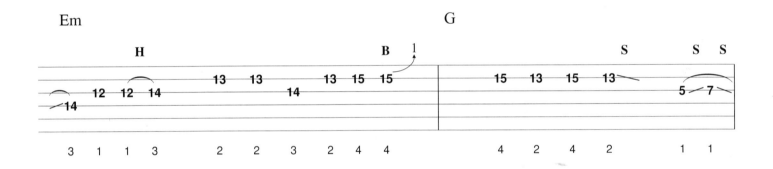

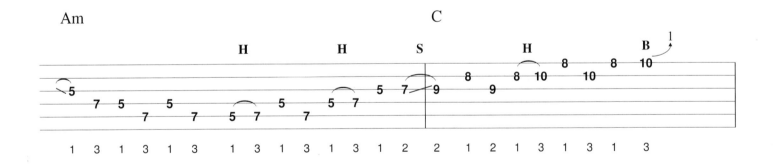

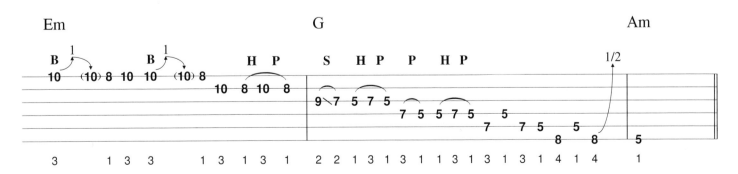

Barre Chord Rhythm & Lead

The second progression of this lesson is a very popular rock rhythm in the key of A minor that uses all barre chords. Since all of the chords are moveable chords, you can also transpose this entire progression to any other key. The four chords used in the key of A minor are shown in the chord diagrams below. The rhythm is straight eighth notes and should be played using all downstrums to get that heavy rock feel. Once you're comfortable changing from one barre chord to the next, you'll be able to transpose the chords and play comfortably in any key.

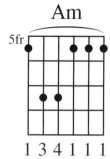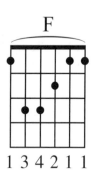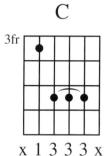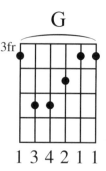

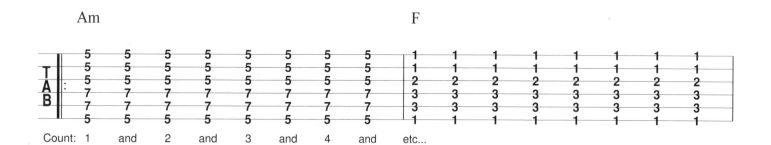

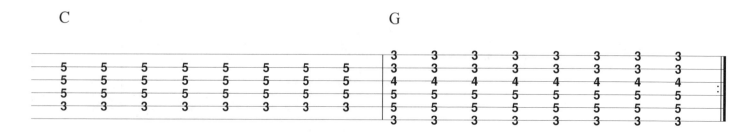

The following example lead can be played over the Barre Chord Rhythm. This solo uses hammer ons and pull offs in combination, slides, various bending techniques and vibrato. The lead starts off in the 1st position A minor pentatonic scale and then shifts up to the 2nd position and then to the 3rd position. Follow the suggested fingerings underneath the tab staff to see some examples of how to switch from one position to the next.

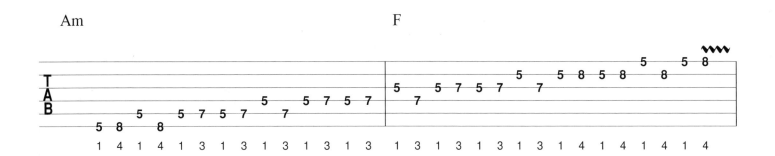

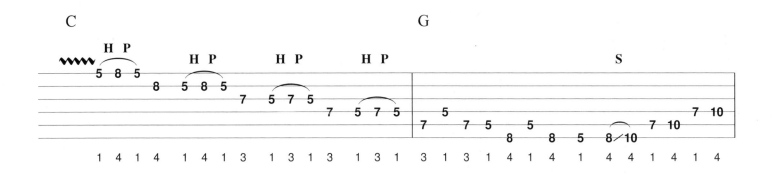

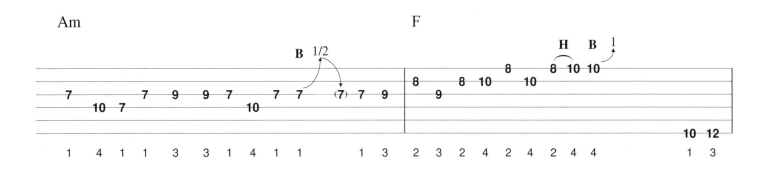

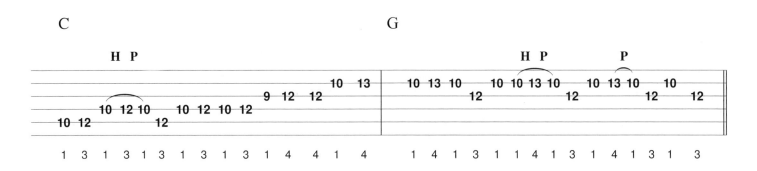

Review Quiz #1

Identify Each Chord

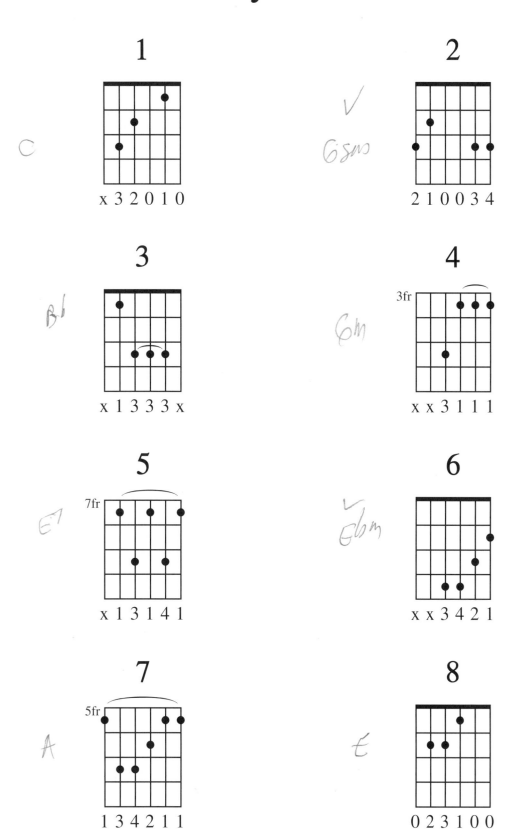

1

C

x 3 2 0 1 0

2

✓

G sus

2 1 0 0 3 4

3

B♭

x 1 3 3 3 x

4

3fr

Gm

x x 3 1 1 1

5

7fr

E7

x 1 3 1 4 1

6

✓

G♭m

x x 3 4 2 1

7

5fr

A

1 3 4 2 1 1

8

E

0 2 3 1 0 0

Answers to the review quiz are located on page 63.

Lesson 7

Workout Section

The following workout section contains a series of exclusive Rock House finger exercises designed to strengthen specific areas of your playing technique. All of these exercises should be practiced along with a metronome. Start out slowly and build speed gradually. Use alternate picking when required and always be sure to use proper fret hand technique.

The Killer!!

This exercise is designed to work on your left hand coordination. Use consistent alternate picking throughout. Play through the first measure slowly until you memorize the pattern. Notice that all four fingers of the left hand are used in succession. For each consecutive measure, the pattern moves down one string. The bottom two tab staffs show the pattern in reverse.

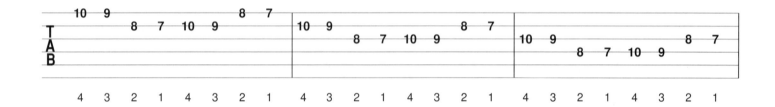

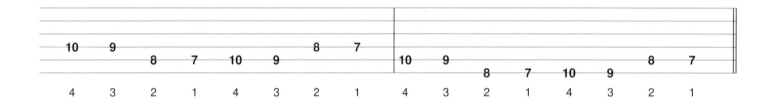

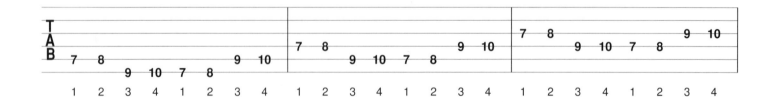

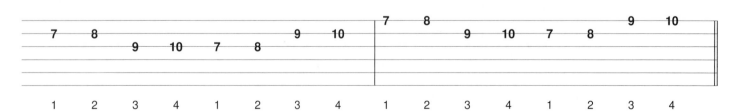

Hammer Rolls

This exercise will help to strengthen the hammer on and pull off techniques. The fingering and fret numbers are the same on each string, and the pattern moves up in groups of three strings for each measure. Play each group of three notes using a smooth triplet feel, picking the first note and hammering on for the next two notes. The second tab staff shows the example in reverse, this time using pull offs and moving down in groups of three strings.

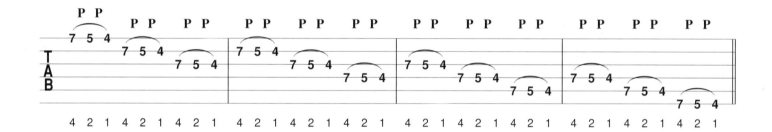

Speed Pick

The Speed Pick exercise is designed to strengthen your picking hand and increase coordination and control of the pick. Practice this exercise using all open strings; you don't need your left hand for this one at all. Follow the picking symbols to get the pattern correct. Repeat each measure for 30 seconds, then repeat the entire exercise for a full five minutes every day. You can practice this anytime, even while relaxing and watching TV.

Finger Crusher

The finger crusher is a left hand workout that will make your fingers stronger and faster. Each section of the exercise starts with a two string pattern from the minor pentatonic scale. Play it four times in position, then move the pattern chromatically (one fret at a time) up the neck to the 12th fret and chromatically back down to where you started at the 5th fret. Your hand will probably get sore and tired before you're even halfway through the exercise, but that just means you're doing it right and getting a great workout. Try to keep time with the metronome and make it your goal to get through the entire exercise without stopping.

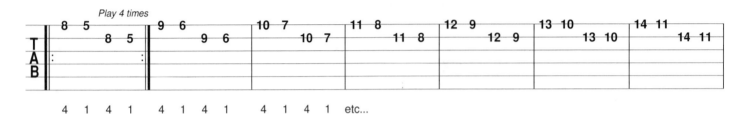

4 1 4 1   4 1 4 1   4 1 4 1   etc...

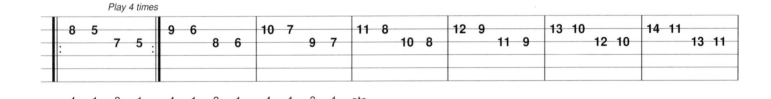

4 1 3 1   4 1 3 1   4 1 3 1   etc...

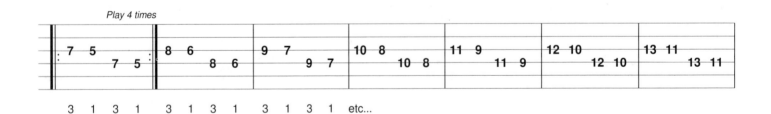

3 1 3 1   3 1 3 1   3 1 3 1   etc...

Play 4 times

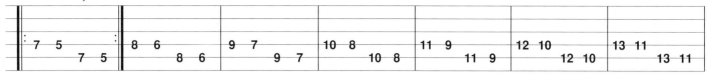

3 1 3 1   3 1 3 1   3 1 3 1   etc...

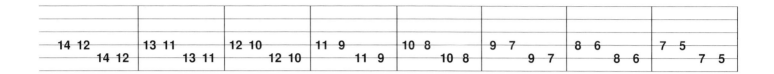

Play 4 times

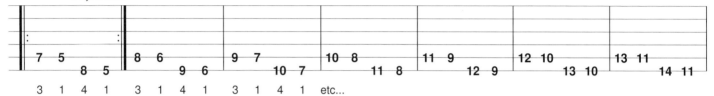

3 1 4 1   3 1 4 1   3 1 4 1   etc...

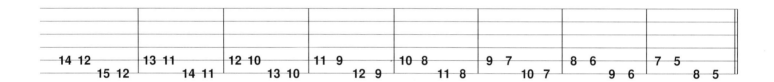

One Hand Rolls

Here's an exercise designed to strengthen your left hand using a series of hammer ons and pull offs.
Pick the very first note of the exercise, then all of the notes should be produced by the left hand only;
don't use the pick at all for the rest of the notes. Your right hand can be used to mute the other strings.

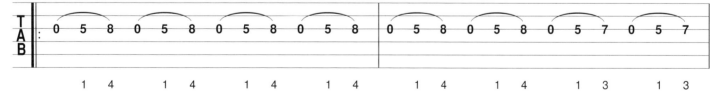

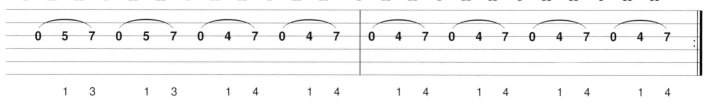

Lesson 8

Blues Rhythm & Lead

This is a standard I - IV - V blues progression in the key of E. The chords are all basic two note chords. Use all downpicking and play the rhythm using a shuffle feel. Once you've got it memorized play along with the bass and drum backing track to get the shuffle feel mastered.

E

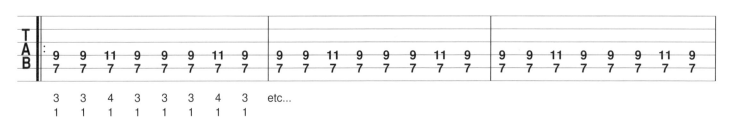

A

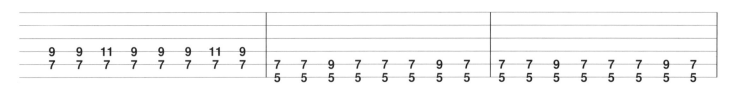

E   B

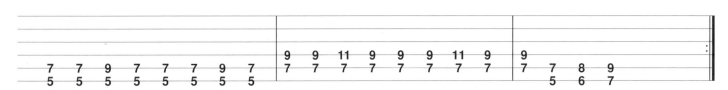

A   E   A A♯ B

You can play the following lead over the Blues Rhythm for an example of how to solo using the pentatonic scales in E. All of the basic lead techniques we've covered so far are represented here. Remember to use a shuffle feel when playing blues solos and riffs.

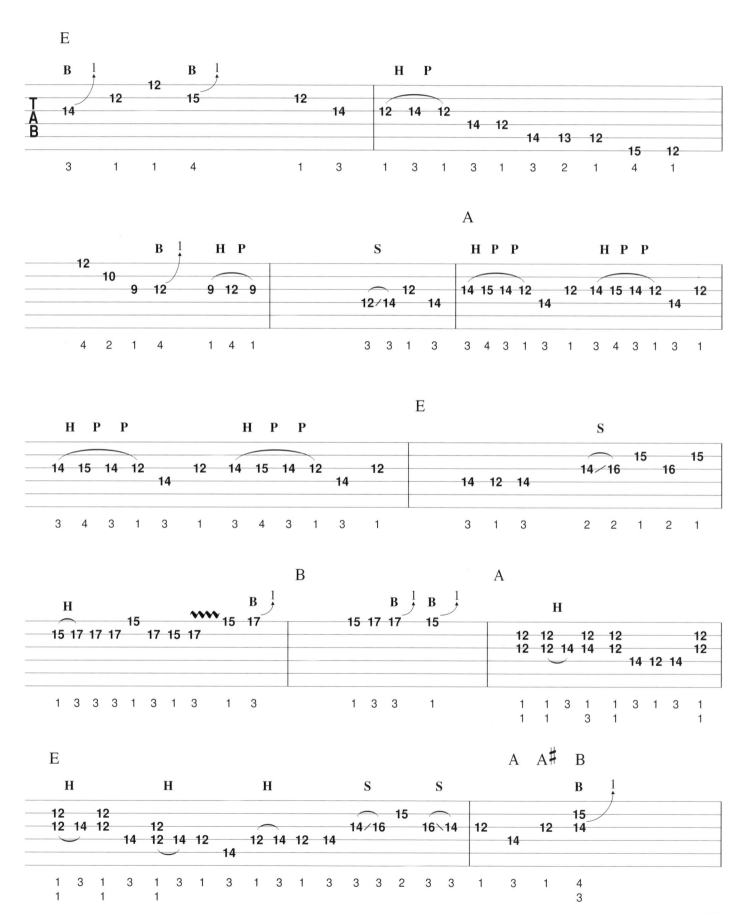

E

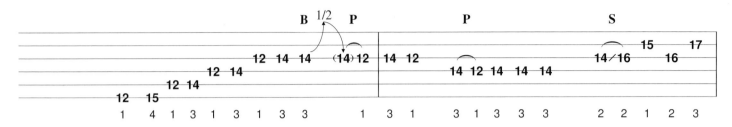

A

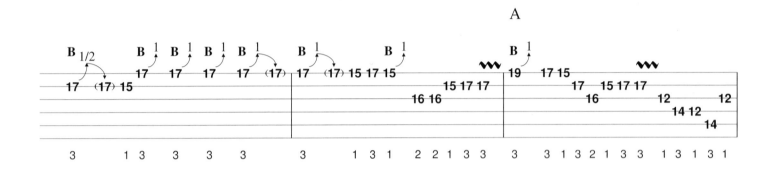

E

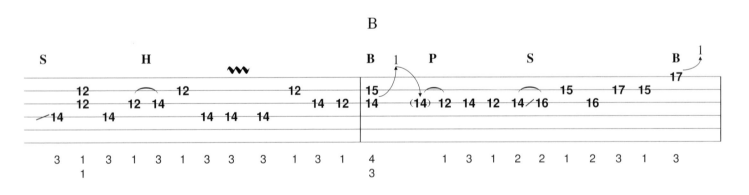

B

A   E   A A# B

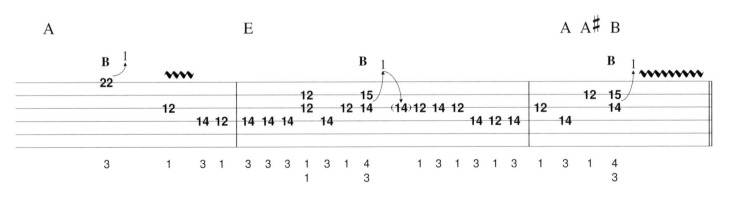

Lesson 9

Blues Scales

The blues scale is a slight variation of the minor pentatonic scale. It contains one extra note between the 4th and 5th steps of the scale, called a *passing tone*. This particular passing tone is the flatted fifth of the scale, also known as the *blues tri-tone*. Using the blues tri-tone adds color and character to solos and riffs. This note is a chromatic passing tone because it passes from the 4th to the 5th steps of the scale in chromatic half steps. Passing tones are used to connect from note to note within a phrase and are generally not held for long durations.

The following five scale positions of the E blues scale are the same as the E minor pentatonic scale with the addition of the blues tri-tone. The Xs in the scale diagrams to the right indicate where the blues tri-tones are played. Practice and memorize the E blues scale positions; we'll be using these scales to play solos in many of the following sections.

1st Position A Blues Scale

1st position

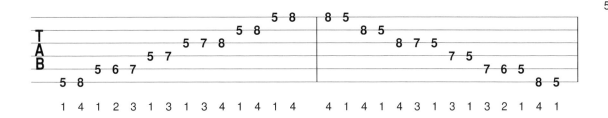

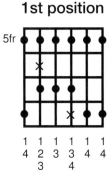

2nd Position A Blues Scale

2nd position

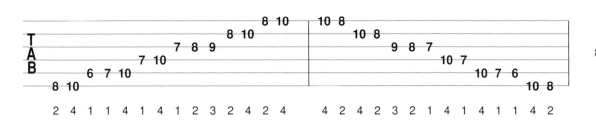

3rd Position A Blues Scale

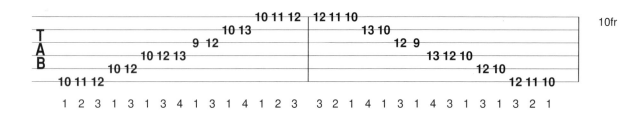

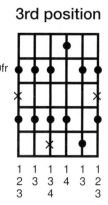

3rd position

4th Position A Blues Scale

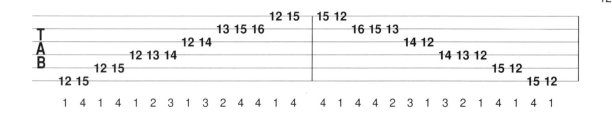

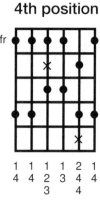

4th position

5th Position A Blues Scale

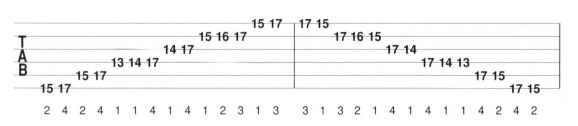

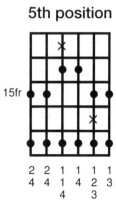

5th position

Lesson 10

Arpeggios

An arpeggio is defined as the notes of a chord played separately. Major and minor arpeggios contain three different name notes: the *root note* (which is the same note as the arpeggio or chord's letter name), the *third* (which is the third scale step and letter name up from the root note), and the *fifth* (the fifth scale step and letter name up from the root note). Full major and minor chords on the guitar are actually groups of root notes, thirds and fifths in different octaves that your hand can reach within that position. Once you know the theory behind which individual notes belong in the chord and where they are on the fretboard, you can create your own chords. More information on arpeggio and chord theory can be found at www.rockhousemethod.com and in the Learn Rock Guitar Advanced program.

Major Arpeggio

The following examples are two octave A major arpeggios. In the first example, follow the picking symbols and use normal, consistent alternate picking.

Alternate Picking

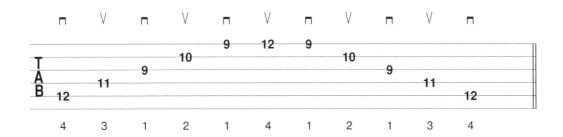

Now try the same A major arpeggio using the *sweep picking* technique. Sweep picking is performed by dragging the pick across the strings in one smooth, flowing motion. In the example below, sweep downward with the pick across the ascending part of the arpeggio. Play the three notes on the 1st string using a combination hammer on and pull off and then sweep back up across the strings with the pick using the same smooth motion. Sweep picking is a very useful technique for playing fast arpeggio runs. The downward sweep picking motion is also referred to as *raking*. This technique may be indicated in music and tablature using the word "rake" followed by a dashed line.

Sweep Picking

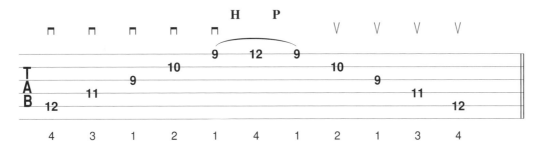

Minor Arpeggio

Here are the A minor arpeggios using alternate picking and sweep picking. Just like with full chords, major arpeggios have a happy or bright tone, while minor arpeggios have a sad or melancholy tone.

Alternate Picking

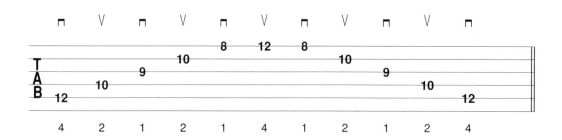

Sweep Picking

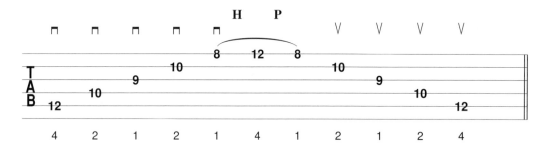

Notice there is only a small difference between the major and minor arpeggios. All of the thirds in the minor arpeggios are one fret (or one half step) lower than the thirds in the major arpeggio. This slight difference is what makes a chord or an arpeggio either major or minor. These notes are also referred to as *major thirds* or *minor thirds*.

Major Arpeggio

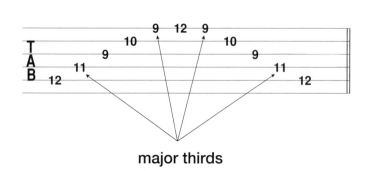

major thirds

Minor Arpeggio

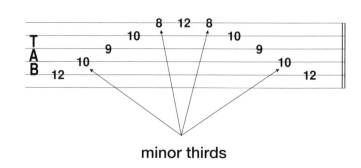

minor thirds

Lesson 11

Rock Rhythm & Melodic Lead

Rock Rhythm

This is a simple rock rhythm that you can play along with the bass and drum backing track (also available on the Lesson Support Site). Follow the count below the tab staff the get the rhythm. When you've got it down, proceed to the following page for a melodic riff that you can play over this progression.

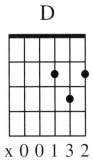

D

x 0 0 1 3 2

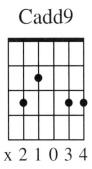

Cadd9

x 2 1 0 3 4

G

2 1 0 0 3 4

D

⊓ ⊓ V   V ⊓ V

```
T  |   2   2   2     2   2   2   2   2   2     2   2   2   3   3   3     3   3   3   3   3   3     3   3   3
   |   3   3   3     3   3   3   3   3   3     3   3   3   3   3   3     3   3   3   3   3   3     3   3   3
A  |:  2   2   2     2   2   2   2   2   2     2   2   2   0   0   0     0   0   0   0   0   0     0   0   0
   |   0   0   0     0   0   0   0   0   0     0   0   0   2   2   2     2   2   2   2   2   2     2   2   2
B  |   0   0   0     0   0   0   0   0   0     0   0   0   3   3   3     3   3   3   3   3   3     3   3   3
```

1   2 and (3) and 4 and etc...

Cadd9

G

```
   |   3   3   3     3   3   3   3   3   3     3   3   3   2   2   2     2   2   2   2   2   2     2   2   2
   |   3   3   3     3   3   3   3   3   3     3   3   3   3   3   3     3   3   3   3   3   3     3   3   3
   |   0   0   0     0   0   0   0   0   0     0   0   0   2   2   2     2   2   2   2   2   2     2   2   2
   |   0   0   0     0   0   0   0   0   0     0   0   0   0   0   0     0   0   0   0   0   0     0   0   0
   |   2   2   2     2   2   2   2   2   2     2   2   2   0   0   0     0   0   0   0   0   0     0   0   0
   |   3   3   3     3   3   3   3   3   3     3   3   3
```

D

Melodic Lead

The following melodic riff within the repeat signs contains *repeat brackets*. The first time the riff is played, you should play the two measures underneath the 1st ending bracket. When the riff is repeated, skip the two measures underneath the 1st ending bracket and continue directly to the measues underneath the 2nd ending bracket.

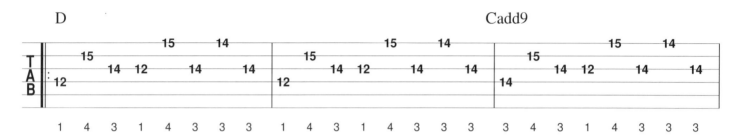

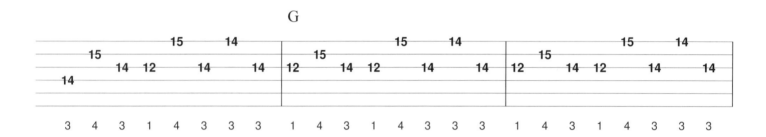

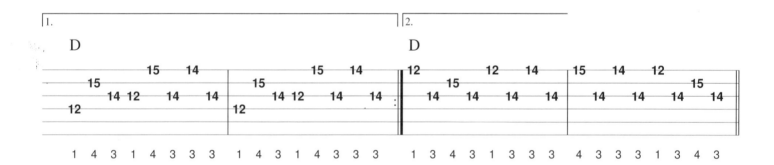

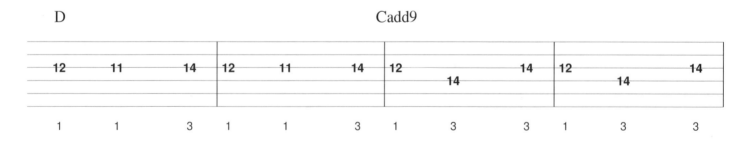

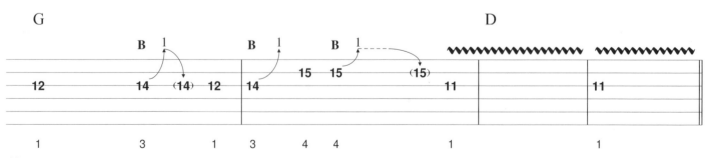

Review Quiz #2

1) How many different positions of the minor pentatonic scale are there?
    A. six
    B. three
    C. five
    D. seven

2) The fast shaking of a sustained note is called
    A. bending
    B. a hammer on
    C. vibrato
    D. a barre

3) Barre chords are
    A. moveable chords
    B. easy to play
    C. open string chords
    D. only used in jazz

4) Two frequently used lead techniques are
    A. tuning and strumming
    B. barre chords and open chords
    C. hammer ons and pull offs
    D. eighth notes and quarter notes

5) Which positions of the minor pentatonic scales can be used for playing leads?
    A. none of them
    B. the 4th and 5th positions
    C. all five positions
    D. only the 1st position

6) Blues scales contain
    A. the blues tri-tone
    B. nine different notes
    C. only open strings
    D. three barre chords

7) An arpeggio is defined as
    A. a scale
    B. a note that is played using vibrato
    C. the notes of a chord played separately
    D. the root note and the seventh

8) The note that makes a chord major or minor is
    A. the fifth
    B. the root note
    C. the third
    D. the seventh

Answers to the review quiz are located on page 63.

Lesson 12

Multi-Position Lead Pattern

This lead pattern uses the A minor pentatonic scale played as a triplet lead pattern across three positions of the scale. This exercise demonstrates various ways to switch from position to position. The first two staffs show the pattern ascending; the bottom two staffs show the same pattern in reverse. Play through each example along with the metronome without stopping and gradually build up speed.

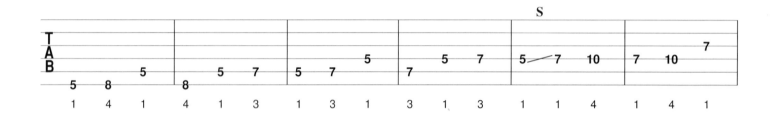

Lesson 13

Bi-Dextral Hammer Ons

This technique introduces the right hand tap, which requires you to reach over to the neck with your right hand and hammer on the note using your right hand index or middle finger. After tapping the note, pull off with your right hand finger to the lower notes on the neck that should be fretted with your left hand fingers. The "R" above the tab staff indicates a right hand tap. This technique allows you to hammer on and pull off full arpeggios and other wide interval phrases very quickly. Right hand tapping was made popular by Eddie Van Halen, who used tapping throughout many of his famous solos.

If you tap with your middle finger, you can keep the pick in position in your hand. If you feel more comfortable tapping with your index finger, you can use a technique called "palming the pick" where you tuck the pick under your middle finger to get it out of the way. After playing the riff, bring it back into position to go back to regular picking.

The following riff is an example of what you can do with bi-dextral hammer ons. Once you're comfortable with the technique, experiment with it at different frets and on different strings. You can also do other fun things with this technique, such as bending a note in your left hand and then tapping a note above it while holding the bend. This bend and tap technique was made popular by Billy Gibbons.

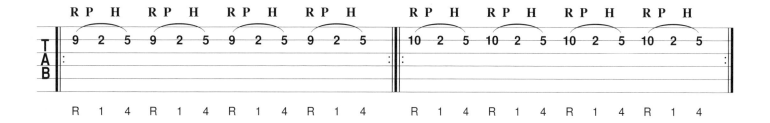

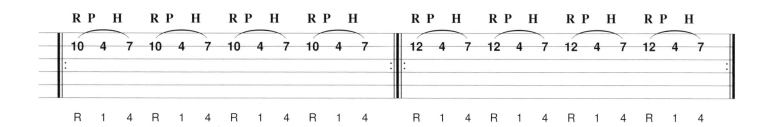

Lesson 14

Natural Minor Scales

Many modern Rock and Blues players have incorporated the use of full natural minor scales into their soloing. The pentatonic scales you've already learned are abbreviated versions of the regular major and minor scales. The pentatonic scales contain five notes; the natural minor scale contains seven notes. The word "natural" refers to the fact that the scale is in its original unaltered state. The A natural minor scale is particularly unique because this key contains all natural notes (no sharp or flat notes). The notes in an A natural minor scale are A - B - C - D - E - F - G. The natural minor scale can be used to create more complex and interesting melodies.

Below are the five basic positions of the A natural minor scale shown ascending and descending. The root notes have all been circled on the staff and scale diagrams.

1st Position A Minor Scale

1st position

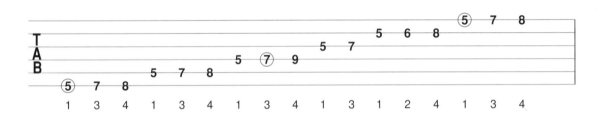

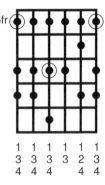

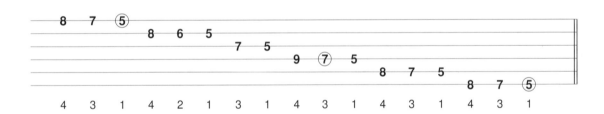

2nd Position A Minor Scale

2nd position

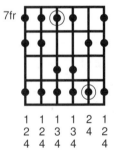

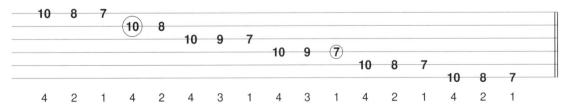

46

3rd Position A Minor Scale

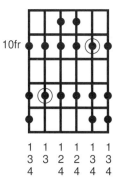

3rd position

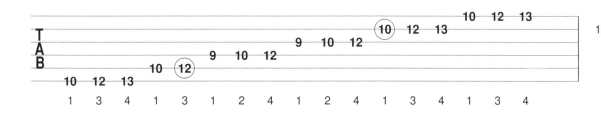

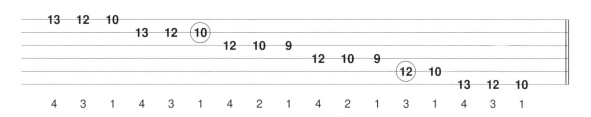

4th Position A Minor Scale

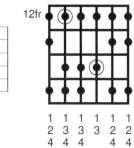

4th position

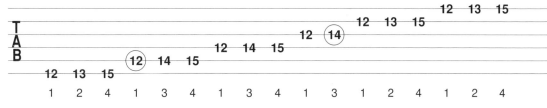

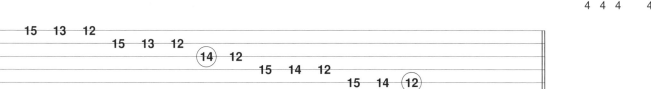

5th Position A Minor Scale

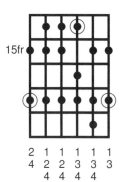

5th position

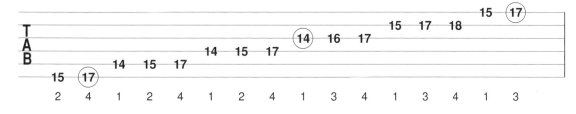

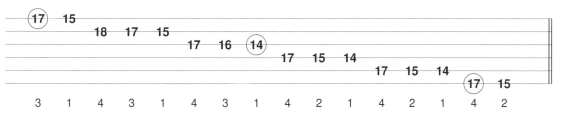

Lesson 15
Drop D Tuning

Drop D tuning refers to lowering the pitch of the 6th string from E to D. This gives the guitar a heavier, meaner sound. Drop D has been used for years in hard rock and heavy metal, so much so that many bands have written their entire catalogs in Drop D.

To tune your guitar to Drop D tuning, strike the open 4th string (D) and the open 6th string together. Gradually lower the 6th string from E to D until the 4th and 6th strings sound "in tune" with each other. These two strings are now both tuned to D an octave apart from each other. You can check your tuning using the online tuner at www.rockhousemethod.com to make sure you've got it.

Rhythms are extremely easy to play in Drop D because the 6th string power chords are now played with just one finger. Simply barre one finger across the lowest three strings at any fret. You can also play a D5 chord just by strumming the lowest three open strings. Below are three chord diagrams to give you some ideas on how to use Drop D tuning to play chords.

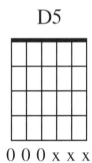

D5

0 0 0 x x x

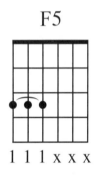

F5

1 1 1 x x x

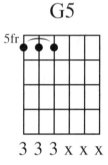

G5

3 3 3 x x x

The following rhythm is a popular heavy metal style riff in Drop D tuning. Play along with the heavy metal bass and drum backing track and get comfortable with the syncopated chord change. Try muting the strings by lightly touching the side of your picking hand against the strings right after the strings come off the bridge. If you move too far away from the bridge, you'll end up deadening the strings instead of getting the proper muted sound. This technique is called *palm muting* and is common in rock and metal. After you've got this example down, experiment and create your own rhythms and riffs in Drop D tuning.

```
  D5          F5          G5          D5          F5          G5
T
A ||: 0   0   0   3   3   3   5   5 | 0   0   0   3   3   3   5   5
B     0   0   0   3   3   3   5   5 | 0   0   0   3   3   3   5   5
      0   0   0   3   3   3   5   5 | 0   0   0   3   3   3   5   5


  D5          F5          G5          D5
      0   0   0   3   3   3   5   5 | 0   0   0   0   0   0   0   0  :
      0   0   0   3   3   3   5   5 | 0   0   0   0   0   0   0   0
      0   0   0   3   3   3   5   5 | 0   0   0   0   0   0   0   0
```

You can solo over the rhythm you've just learned using the minor pentatonic scales in the key of D. Since the 6th string is tuned down to D, all of the 6th string notes in the scale positions have moved two frets. To avoid confusion and mistakes, you can simply avoid playing notes on the 6th string. It's also good to remember that since you are in the key of D and your 6th string is now tuned to D, the open string and the 12th fret notes are now root notes that you can easily use as well.

The following example solo uses the D minor pentatonic scale in various positions. The position changes are indicated below the staff as they happen.

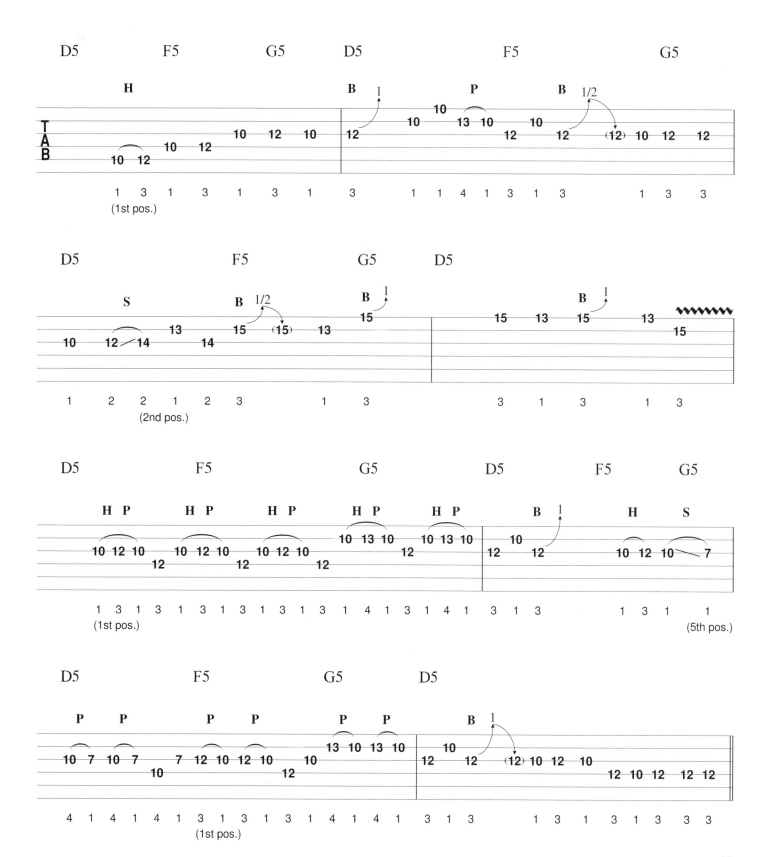

49

Lesson 16
Slow Metal Rhythm & Solo

This slow metal rhythm is an arpeggiated riff in the key of Bm. Keep your left hand fingers in place, fretting the notes throughout each measure and let the notes ring out over each other as you pick them. The picking rhythm is straight eighth notes with a slow, simple feel. Once you've got the pattern memorized, play along with the bass and drum backing track.

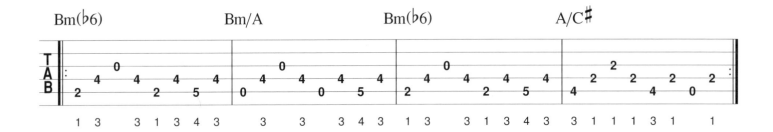

The following solo demonstrates various lead techniques learned throughout this program and can be played over the Slow Metal Rhythm. This lead is in the key of Bm and uses different positions of the B natural minor scale. You can also improvise your own lead using the B minor scales. All of the A natural minor scale positions from Lesson 14 can be transposed to the key of Bm by moving each of them two frets higher on the fretboard.

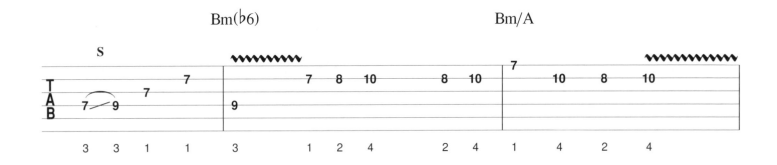

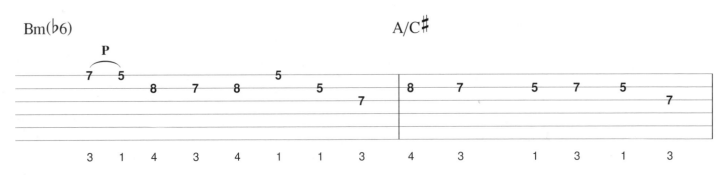

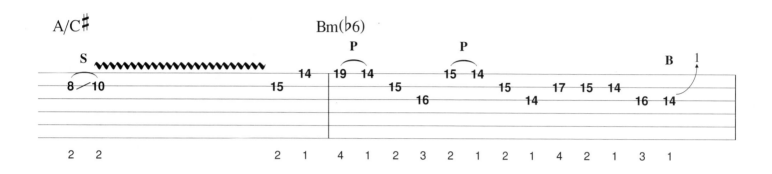

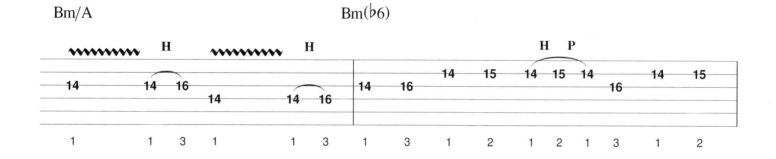

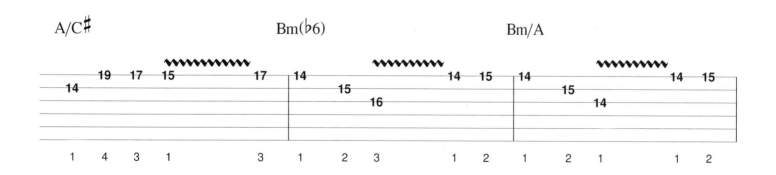

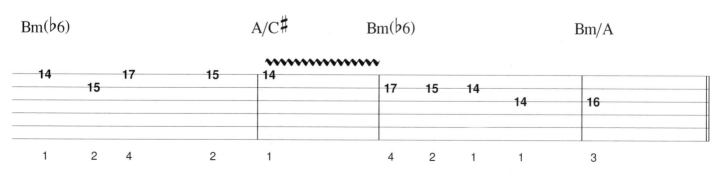

Review Quiz #3

1) The bi-dextral hammer on technique requires you to
   A. switch hands and play the guitar upside down
   B. fret all of the notes with your left hand
   C. reach over to the neck and tap notes with your right hand
   D. use distortion

2) Right hand tapping is indicated by which letter above the tab staff?
   A. B
   B. R
   C. S
   D. H

3) When tapping with your right hand index finger, move the pick out of the way by
   A. palming the pick
   B. dropping the pick
   C. putting the pick down
   D. holding the pick between your teeth

4) How many different letter name notes are in the natural minor scale
   A. five
   B. three
   C. eight
   D. seven

5) To play in Drop D tuning,
   A. use a distortion pedal
   B. drop D guitar on D floor
   C. tune the guitar's 6th string down to D
   D. tune every string on the guitar to D

6) You can fret power chords in Drop D tuning by using how many fingers?
   A. five
   B. one
   C. four
   D. seven

7) Transpose the A natural minor scale positions to the key of B minor by moving each position
   A. two frets higher
   B. two frets lower
   C. five frets higher
   D. seven frets lower

8) Which of the following is not a lead technique?
   A. hammer ons
   B. bends
   C. bi-dextral hammer ons
   D. barre chords

Answers to the review quiz are located on page 63.

Guitar Accessories

Strings & Picks

Strings and picks are both available in different gauges. Heavier gauge strings produce a thicker, fuller sound; lighter gauges are thinner, easier to bend, and great for soloing. There are many different types of picks in different thicknesses. A heavy pick may offer you more control for lead playing, but medium and light picks have a flexibility that's good for rhythm playing. A fingerpick is a type of ring that you wear on your thumb for downpicking, allowing all of your fingers to be available for more complex fingerpicking. When changing your strings, you'll probably want to use a string winder. A string winder is a simple gadget that fits right over the machine heads so that you can quickly wind or unwind a string.

Strings come in various styles and gauges.

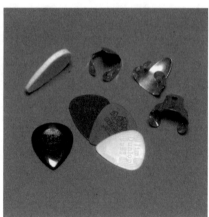

Different types of picks are available.

String winders make changing strings easier.

Music Stands & Metronomes

As soon as you begin your first guitar lesson, you'll notice how important it is to have a music stand. Whenever you try to learn a new song from sheet music, or even go through a lesson in this book, you'll want to have the music right in front of you where it's close and easy to read. Don't try to balance a book on your lap or read it from the floor. If you're practicing scales and exercises or working out a difficult new guitar line, you can use a metronome to set a steady practice tempo and keep yourself in time. There are mechanical or electronic models, or you can download the free one from www.rockhousemethod.com and use your computer to keep time.

Capos & Slides

A capo is a moveable clamp that attaches to the neck of the guitar and barres across all six strings. Whichever fret the capo is placed at can then be thought of as the nut; the capo transposes the entire guitar to that position, making it possible to play all of the open chords there. Many acoustic players prefer the full open chord sound and use capos almost exclusively. Capos are popular at the 1st, 2nd, 3rd, 5th and 7th frets, but you can place a capo anywhere at all on the neck. A capo at the 12th fret transposes the guitar one octave higher and gives it a bright, mandolin tone.

An essential element of the blues guitar sound is the slide. A slide is a sleeve (usually glass) that fits over the ring finger of your left hand. With a slide you can slide notes or chords in a steady, smooth motion, making the guitar "talk." Slide guitar is also very popular in many rock styles, and can be heard in songs like "Freebird" and "Bad to the Bone."

Capo properly placed at the 2nd fret.

A slide can be worn on your ring finger.

Effects

Effects play an important role in every guitar player's arsenal. There are many different effects and different types of units available for you to experiment with while creating your own signature sounds. You can use foot pedals as well as rack mount effects units. Some basic effects that are useful are distortion, chorus, flangers and phasers, compressors, harmonizers and wah wah pedals.

With newer USB converters and software, you can also plug your guitar into a computer and play your way through cyberspace. Just connect right to your pc and you can get access to a whole arsenal of software featuring guitar effects, amp sounds, interactive lessons and virtual recording studios.

Various guitar effects pedals.

Tuners

An electronic tuner is a necessity for any gigging guitarist, and tuners have become so common that they're often included in other effects units. Tuners are also sometimes put right into a guitar's electronics. If you don't have a tuner, you can download the free online tuner at our support website.

Electronic digital tuner

Straps

Acoustic guitar straps can attach at the body if there's a strap button there. If not, a strap can be tied to the headstock between the nut and the machine heads. Straps come in a variety of materials and styles. When picking out a strap, try to find one that's both comfortable and that looks good with your guitar. Also available are strap locks (locking buttons that will keep the strap secured to the guitar).

Guitar straps

Cords

Investing a few dollars more to get a nice, heavy duty guitar cord is worthwhile. The cheaper ones don't last very long, while a professional quality cable can work perfectly for years. Some of the better cords even include a lifetime warranty. Cords also come in a variety of lengths, gauges and colors.

Guitar cords

Cases & Stands

The two main types of guitar cases are hardshell cases and softshell cases. Hardshell cases are more expensive and have a sturdy construction designed for maximum protection during travel. A much lighter and smaller alternative to the traditional guitar case is a gig bag: a padded, zippered guitar glove that is carried over the shoulders like a backpack. Guitar stands are usually collapsible and easy to take with you, but you can also use one at home to keep your guitar on display when you're not practicing.

Hardshell case

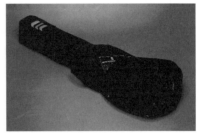
Gig bag

Make Your Own Tool Kit

Put together your own tool kit by keeping all of the important tools and spare parts you need in one place, like a small backpack or a compartment inside your guitar case. You should always have spare strings, a string winder, picks, batteries, and any small screwdrivers or wrenches that fit your guitar. You can purchase a multipurpose tool designed especially for guitarists (sort of like a pocket knife without the knife) that contains a few different types of screwdrivers and an assortment of allen wrenches. Some other good things to keep with you: wire cutters, fuses if your amp uses them, guitar polish and a soft cloth, music paper and pencil, and duct tape. You may also want to keep a small recording device handy to record your own musical ideas and use them to start writing your own songs.

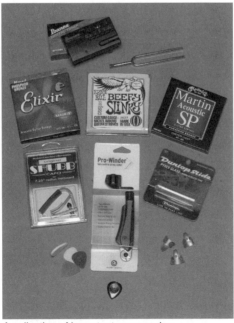
A collection of important accessories.

Guitar Solo
from Learn Rock Guitar Intermediate DVD

This solo is an inspirational piece that contains many of the scales and techniques that are taught in my Learn Rock Guitar Beginner, Intermediate, and Advanced programs. When trying to learn a challenging piece you should break it down into small sections, mastering each before moving to the next. I hope you enjoy your musical journey.

- John McCarthy

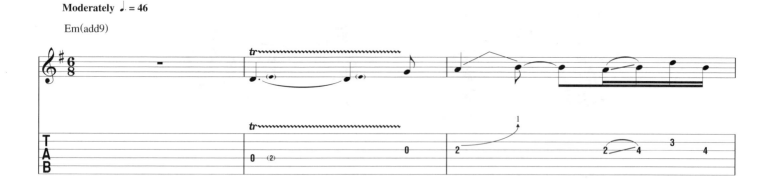

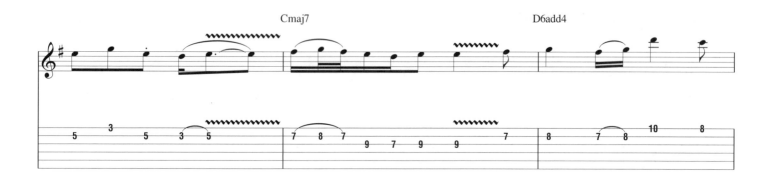

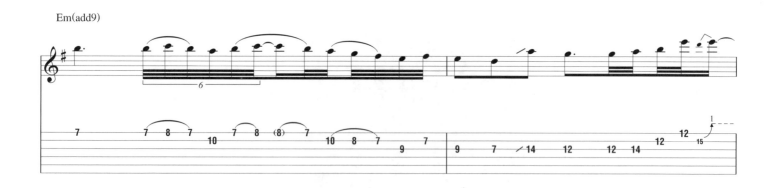

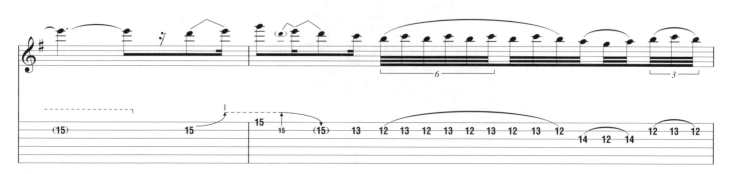

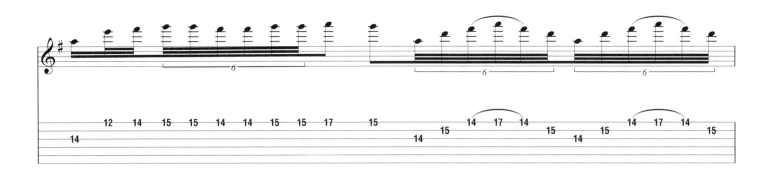

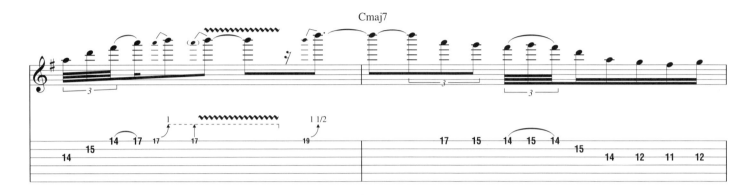

Cmaj7

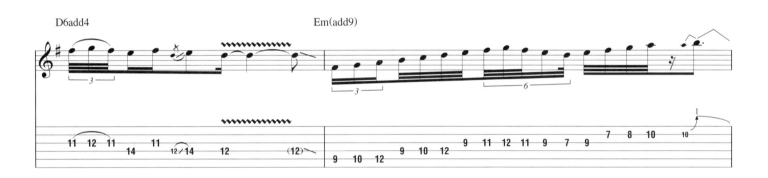

D6add4   Em(add9)

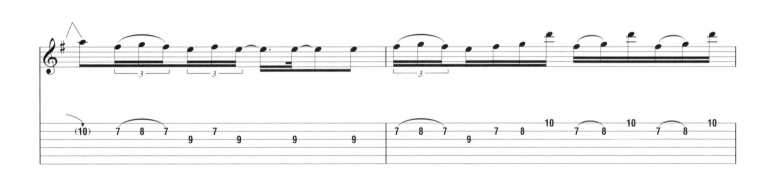

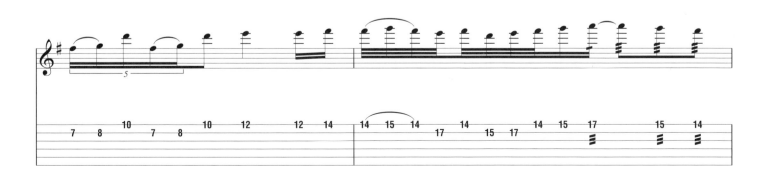

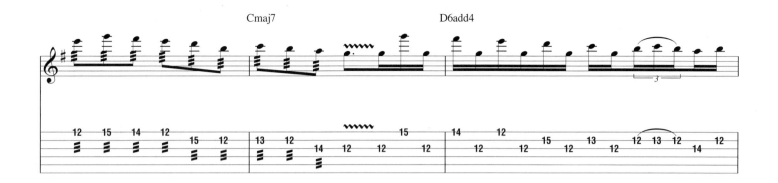

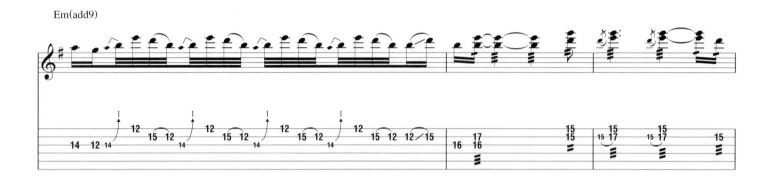

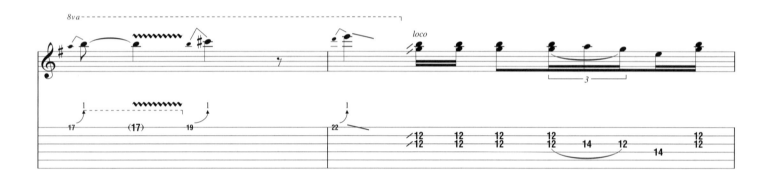

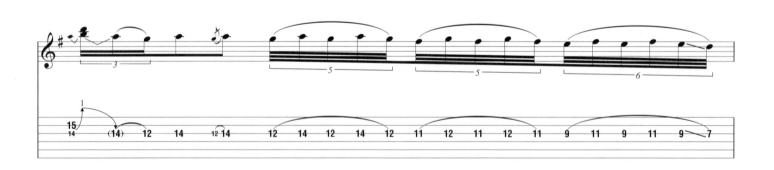

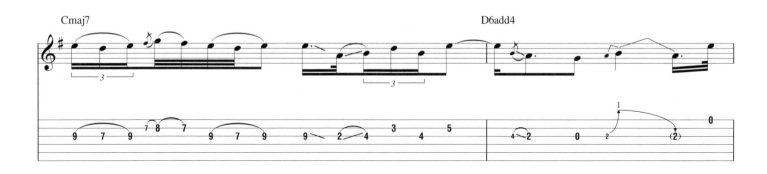

Em(add9)

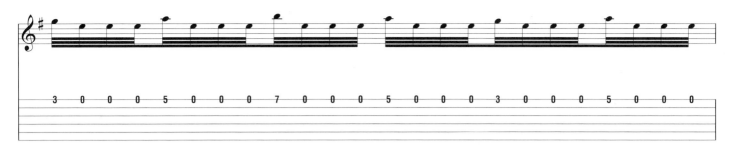

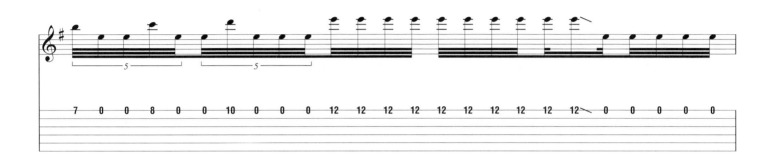

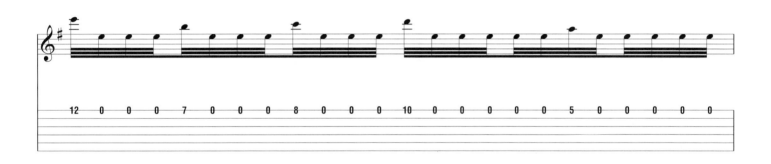

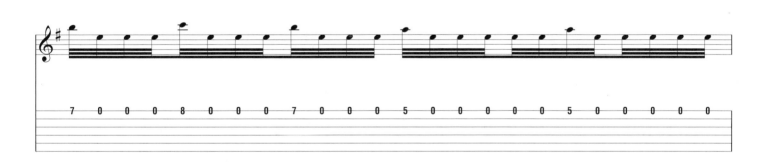

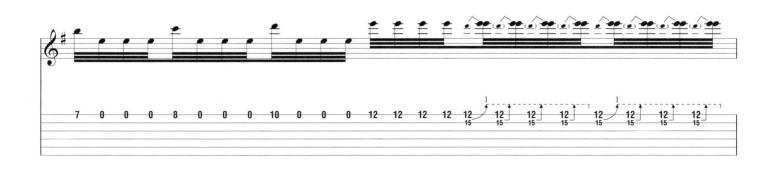

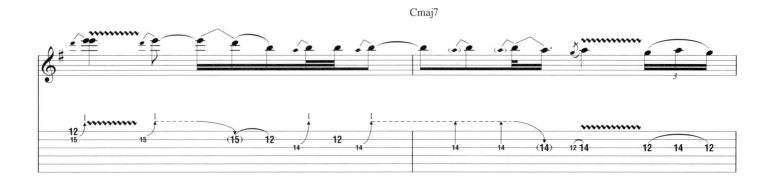

Cmaj7

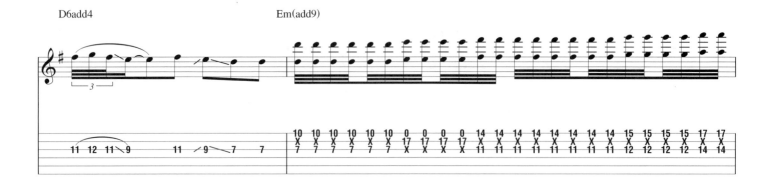

D6add4   Em(add9)

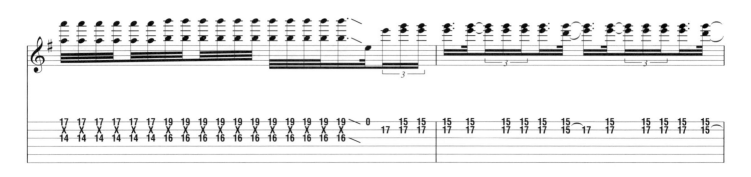

Begin fade   *Fade out*

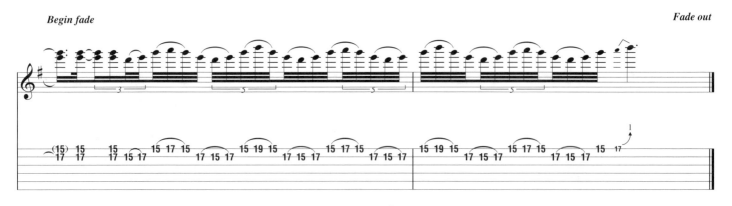

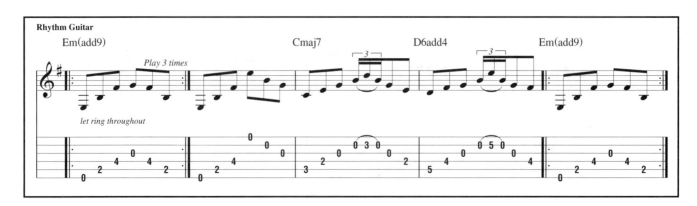

62

Learn Rock Guitar Intermediate
CD track list & page index

Review Quiz Answer Key

Review Quiz #1

1) C

2) G

3) B♭

4) Gm

5) E7

6) Bm

7) A

8) E

Review Quiz #2

1) C

2) C

3) A

4) C

5) C

6) A

7) C

8) C

Review Quiz #3

1) C

2) B

3) A

4) D

5) C

6) B

7) A

8) D